# Uncaged Wallflower

## Extended Edition

D1502116

By Jennae Cecelia

Uncaged Wallflower
Extended Edition

ISBN: 978-1548743130

Illustrations by Rylie Moran
Instagram: @gabriellescrapart

Cover art by Islam Farid
www.IslamFarid.net

This book is a work of fiction. Names, characters, places, and incidents are products of the author's imagination or are used factiously. Any resemblance to actual events of locales or persons, living or dead, is entirely coincidental.

Jennae Cecelia

*Dear Reader,*

Rather than speaking my mind right away, I was always more of a quiet thinker. I was an introvert. A wallflower.

To add to this, my mind was conjuring up negative thoughts I let flow out of my mouth with ease, ignoring the positive outlook I could have if only I could stop focusing on my flaws.

I wrote **Uncaged Wallflower** for those who feel trapped in the thoughts their minds produce, unable to express them with the rest of the world out of fear of critique or disagreement.

This is for those who need an extra dose of positivity in their day and a push to follow their dreams.

This is not a poetry book for you to read and relate to in a sorrow filled way. It is for you to read and say, *"yes, I can be better and I will."*

So please, don't ever feel like your opinion is less important than the opinion of others. Don't let your insecurities and anxious mind dictate your bliss. Never stop being a dreamer.

With love,
Jennae

Reading a book is reading
someone's story;
their heart,
their mind,
their soul.
This is mine for you.

Happiness is a choice,
and when you choose it
you will find it,
even when the nights
are pitch black
and the days are cloudy.

*-I choose happiness*

Metamorphosis.
Feeling your wings
break through.
Growing into the best you.
Emerge from
your chrysalis.
Expand and learn
something new.
Don't get wrapped up in
your same old cocoon.

## *Live Your Life*

How long are you
going to **live**
your life
for other people?
Answering calls for them.
Emails piling **your** inbox
with nothing but
bitching and moaning.
Making coffee runs
for six other people.
Curling your hair
instead of leaving it straight
because people told you
that you looked better
that way.
Pressing makeup brushes
to your face
because somehow it
became out of the norm to
show up to work
or events with
your bare face.
Because, *how dare you*
for showing your true colors.
How long are you going
to live your **life**
for other people?
Stop conforming to the norm.

It's hard to say *yes*
when the voice of anxiety
screams *no.*
But this world
offers too much to not
explore out of fear.
I'm still learning to live
outside of my comfort zone.

*-shut up, anxiety*

Some flowers
are tempting to pick
and take with us for our
own selfish reasons,
but they are most beautiful
and will flourish more
when left in their natural form.
Kind of like you.

Ask yourself this:
*if not you, then who?*
Someone has to be that
doctor,
or musician,
or chef.
No dream is too small.
No job is too big.

**-you are a boss babe**

If you put a fraction
of the love
you give to everyone else
into yourself,
you would never doubt
your purpose again.

*-you deserve your own love*

I wonder how our souls are
picked for our bodies.
Is a good soul placed into a
bad body just to show others
not to judge by outer appearance?
Or, is a rotten soul put into a
beautiful body
to show others that looks are
only enough
until times get tough?
Either way, our souls are what
we take from this life to the next
and our body is what is laid to
rest.

Jennae Cecelia

## *No More Tomorrow*

If it's not yesterday,
it's tomorrow,
or next week,
or next year.
I find myself living in thoughts
of the future more than
the realities of the present.
Hurrying through weekly tasks with
thoughts only embedded with
weekend bliss.
Contemplating if I said the right thing,
or if there was anything I missed.
I have to remind myself that I am
wasting present moments thinking
of a future that will either
come or not,
but that's out of my control.
So, I take brief moments,
sit and enjoy the stars
and the way the grass
moves in the wind.
Because those are present moments
and I need to exist there more.

You may think
you are caged in
with little room
for growth,
but to every lock
there is a key.

And that's the thing
about people.
You can wrap them up
in kindness & love,
and they will still have
something cold to say
about you.

## Change

I have always hated change.
Even as a child I would
become frustrated
when the store would move
the aisle of dolls
to a different location
than before.
**I hated** when trees were
torn down and a large empty
space filled the home they
once owned.
**I hated** when the walls were painted
a new color and I would never
see the hue beneath it again.
**I hated** not being able to
adapt to change
as quickly as others.
But change is all around us.
We are always getting older,
looking older.
The building built five years ago
will need repairs.
And sometimes I wonder
if landfills are piled
with all the changes people made.
Discarded items they lost attachment
to or needed to part with in order
to move on.
Change is always there.
Embrace the growth you are making.

Discard the rest.
Learn that change may bother
you at first,
but it will save you in the end.

## *Moments*

We have finite moments
in an infinite universe.
Some that we count as
our best memories,
and others we suppress.
We are made up of moments.
The pictures hidden
between pages of books.
The concert tickets piling up
in a bin,
crinkled from when we shoved
them in our pockets and then
washed the jeans.
Life is beautiful for giving us
these moments.
We may be made of
cells,
bones,
and muscle,
but moments are what make up
our souls.
Embrace your moments.
The good and the bad.
Moments come too quickly,
and one day you will do anything
to have them back.

We are broken people.
made up of,
cracks,
rips,
tears,

bruises,
cuts,
and scars.
But only a few choose
to pick up the pieces
and form something new
out of the shattered debris.

There is no such thing
as perfect.
No one is free from faults.
No one is ever going to
always say the right things.
The way we look is not perfect,
because perfect is a figment
humans make up in their
minds from pictures
of "ideal" men and women.

## *Unpredictability*

Fear is attached
to unpredictability.
Fear of an expectation
not being met.
Fear of a momentous
time ending.
But for me,
the best things happened
out of unpredictability.
My mind used to limit my options,
leaving little room for new
ideas or endings.
I would call the unknown and
I best friends now.
Because the unfamiliar is my
path to my next great task.
I wake up with excitement
in my stomach thinking
of all the possibilities ahead.
Here's to living without the fear
of not knowing what is around
the bend.

I used to be envious of
the people who took all the
good kinds of risks.
The ones who packed their
bags and stuffed their car
full of everything they would need
to start over halfway across
the country.
But now I am smiling,
because that person
is someone I could be.

You could hate me with
deep passion
and I'd still love you
with full embrace.
This world just has
too many people
quick to blow you off
for your silly mistakes.

You are hating on your body
that is screaming for
your love.

You ask why we don't
talk like we used to,
and I tell you we do.
The only difference is this time
I'm the one not
answering anymore and
you get to be the one
hanging on to my every
word, hoping for a response.

*-you didn't know how good I was*
*until I was gone*

Go to the top of a hill,
a mountain,
a building,
and scream out
your dream.
Demand for it, and believe in it.
That echo you hear
is the Universe taking note.

Believe that your vision is the
pathway to your success.
No dream is a fantasy until
you let yourself settle with
the thought that it is.
You need to pave a path.
One that many follow.
A trail people continue down
for years to come.
Hatchet in hand to make
clearance of overgrown weeds
and stumps in the way.
A pathway that is run over
with footsteps of curiostiy.
People wondering how you
got to this point.
How you made your vision
a reality,
when it was once only parked
in the depths of your mind.
How you were able to stay
positive and happy
even when you didn't know
exactly when your next
paycheck would come.
Let them wonder how you got
to where you are.
Let them be the ones to try
and follow the path
you have paved.
Grab your hatchet,
and start clearing your path today.

## *Let Me Tell You, You're Beautiful*

At a young age, I felt the need to
protect people.
My soon-to-be friend who was
pushed around by the fourth-grade bully.
Who told her she was dumb,
and ugly.
I was at a loss because I wanted to be
liked by the other kids in class,
but I couldn't help feeling a vast amount of
pain for the girl in the jumpsuit and
red glasses.
She was the outcast and I wanted
to cry right along with her.
As I got older these situations didn't
really change.
Although the settings were no longer
playgrounds or lunchrooms filled with
adolescents,
it was now an office with grown adults
competing for a higher role.
It was the guys at the bar on a Saturday night,
laughing at the girls with a little extra weight
who were just trying to enjoy drinks
without stares of disgust.
It was the women being cheated on
because the temptation was too strong
for their unfaithful men.
I feel people's pain, and I want to rescue them.
I want to tell them they are better than
the images people have of them.
That they are beautiful.

Jennae Cecelia

## *Shadows*

The shadows looming in
the corners wore colors
similar to bruises.
No way of knowing
when the darkness would end.
Heart racing in your chest.
Staccato breaths.
Sweat staining your palms.
Darkness came in random spouts.
Dripping slowly,
or rushing fast.
Hot or cold,
it was never known.
Oh, how darkness could find you.
Darkness could find you knee deep
in happiness and come slap you
back into the reality of the hate.
Run fast, my friend.
Don't let the darkness catch you today.
Don't let the darkness overtake.

She knew the universe
had a lot to offer,
but she didn't realize
the universe was part of her too.

*-she is the sun, moon, and stars*

You are never going to find
your own voice
while trying to match
the pitch of everyone else's.

*-be a rare composition*

## Change Is Inevitable

I thought I would go
to a four-year college
a couple states away.
I thought I would have roommates
and attend parties
I would only pretend to like.
I thought I would eat bland cafeteria food
and shower around 10-15 other girls.
I thought I would study in my 12x12 room
under a desk lamp,
and walk to and from class all day.
I thought my weekends would be filled
with late nights with friends that would
one day be the bridesmaids
in my wedding.
These were things I wanted.
Instead, I went to college ten minutes
from my house.
My roommates were my parents,
and the only "parties" I had on the weekends
were drinking wine and watching
some overly dramatic *Lifetime* movie
with my mom.
I ate food that was handed out drive-thru
windows or cooked on the stove
in my kitchen.
I studied occasionally but mostly just
relied on my good memory to help me
pass my classes.
The reality is,

I thought a lot of things
at the age of 18.
And the way things
turned out at that time,
I thought were disappointing.
But now, I am grateful
I didn't get all the things
I wanted.
I am glad I was different
from most of my peers.
Be open to different things.
Bumps in the road
may actually be
exactly the alteration
you need.
Change is inevitable,
but it is up to you
to grow with it
and make it as ideal
as you can.

I was the candle that stayed lit
even in the
d
o
w
n
pour of rain.
The flame, never getting weak
from outside pressure.
I will never decrease my fire
that everyone tries to put out.
They are just afraid the light
inside of me might destroy them.

## *My Path To You*

In life,
you are given
paths to choose.
Some are perfectly paved
with flowers
and directions
at each bend.
Others have
overgrown grass
with dirt
and no definite map.
Each brings forth
adventures,
excitement,
or dead ends.
Follow each path
with passion
because you don't know
where you could be lead.
Of all the paths
I have gone down
with bumps,
sharp turns,
dead ends,
and flowers,
my favorite was the one
that lead me to you.

Make a wish on a dandelion.
Blow your dreams into the wind.
The Universe will answer,
you just have to believe.

*-thank you, Universe*

Do you ever have that
feeling deep in your stomach
of worrying about having
to say hello and goodbye
to people as you pass?
Like there is no proper moment
to do so and that you might
stumble over your words.
Or what if they don't
say anything back?
Or what if they are
overly friendly and
want to chat?
Or what if they laugh?

*-social anxiety*

## Cleanse

You can wash the dirt off of your body,
watch as it flows down the drain.
You can wash out your mind
and watch the world
around you change.
Some things happen
in less obvious ways.
That doesn't mean they
aren't still happening.

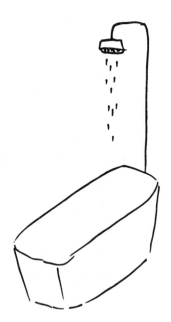

You aren't ugly
because you have some fat.
You aren't pretty
because you show more bone.
You are more than just your shell.
You are your soul.

Surround yourself with people
who don't just ask
how you are doing.
Surround yourself with people
who make an effort to
make sure they are part of
the reason you are doing so well.

## *Villian*

Who told you to be quiet?
Who told you
the best place to be
was off in the corner of the room
as far away from
human interaction
as possible?
Who made you feel like
your words didn't matter?
Who laughed at the thoughts that
you shared
after building up
the courage to speak?
I'm telling you to not be quiet.
Be loud and be known.
Talk to the people who seem
louder than you.
Share the thoughts dancing in
your brain with confidence
and ease.
Whoever told you
that you didn't matter
and neither did your opinion,
I'm encouraging you
to be the hero
taking over that villain.

## *No More Silence*

If you feel like you have to be silent,
let me be the first to say you don't.
And if you want to be quiet,
let me be the first to say that is okay.
But, make sure your silence is your choice
and not because you are scared
of what your voice may say.

Jennae Cecelia

It's the small steps
that guide you to
the biggest dreams.
You just have to
start walking.

## Forgiveness

I used to hold grudges
like a child clinging to their mother
on the first day of kindergarten.
I couldn't let them go.
The things people said to me
were stored in individual files
in my brain marked with their name.
The *things I hate* file bigger than
the *things I love.*
People piling up like scattered
notes on a desk.
The grudges I held becoming
a dark mess.
I started organizing my thoughts.
Filtering out the bad
and pouring in the good.
I learned that I just needed to
forgive and move on.
Even if the people who caused
my negative thoughts never know,
I no longer have a grudge against them,
because I had made forgiveness my home.

You say you want
to explore the world
but you have barely
explored yourself.

### *100%*

You need to **realize** that
you deserve the best.
If the "love" **you** receive
is nothing but deception
and unpredictability,
only to be masked by your
wide eyes
and big heart,
please know you can leave.
Don't use comfort as a reason to stay.
No relationship **should** ever be a
90/10 type of love.
Find someone who gives it their all
and matches your efforts.
Look at the relationship
you **have** right now.
If they aren't giving their **100%**,
it's time for it to end.

### *Killing Fear*

I used to be confined to the comfort,
of my house or bed.
The places I thought couldn't hurt me,
where I hid instead.
From people who took too many glances,
or the chance of having actual fun.
Fear used to consume my whole body,
but I killed fear with freedom
and now fear and I are done.
I now use my bed for sleeping,
and my home as a quick stop
after a busy day.
My head creates thoughts of happiness
instead of playing the same scene over
and over in pain.

Spend time in your mind
with silence surrounding you.
Filter out all the outside
noise that is trying so hard
to change your direction.

You can have
one hundred friends
and still feel so alone
on your venture.
Strive for friends
who call you at midnight
on your birthday,
show up at your house
unexpectedly just to take you
out to lunch,
or let you cry to them
when you lose
an important person.
Have a group that will
run with you through
any season of life.

## *Stars*

Out of all the stars,
you were the one he looked toward
at night.
Never knowing that to him, you shone
brighter than the rest.
Even if there was an overabundance
of bigger or brighter stars,
you were always the one his eyes fell to.
The light he trusted would guide him.
The one he searched for even on
the most overcast of evenings.
I bet if you didn't spend time
comparing your qualities to the others,
you would have felt his eyes
always locked on you.
But remember, he is the one who
knew you shone,
even before you did yourself.

## *It's Okay To Ask Why*

I was envious of the
honor roll students
as I stared at my C's.
I was the student
who needed to ask,
"what" or, "why"
instead of doing the
task with ease.
I later learned there is
nothing wrong with being
the student who raises
your hand with a question
instead of the answer.

Bad moods live dormant in
our bodies waiting for
outside influences to fuel
their intensity.
Learn to control
the flames so they
don't spread like wildfire.

It is bittersweet to
put a friendship to rest
when the person once had a big
impact on your life,
but no longer supports
the person you are
blossoming into.
I promise you,
when you leave behind those
who bring negativity
into your life,
many positive friends will
come pouring in.

*-out with the old, in with the new*

## Express Her Problems

She grew up thinking
strength meant not
being vulnerable.
Putting on her best poker face.
She fought the, "I love myself,
no, I hate myself" blues.
She never understood the people
who would cry at movies.
How could they dare show
such emotion in public?
Didn't they know sobs like that
were meant only for their
pillow?
She thought she was strong
because she didn't show her fears.
Didn't talk about her problems.
Because, if she didn't talk about
her issues, then they didn't exist,
right?
That girl wasn't strong.
She was broken
and torn, a bird slowly
having each feather plucked.
Soon she was going to crash and burn.
She didn't need to bottle up the problems,
because problems weren't meant
to be kept in her head.
One small shake of that bottle
and the explosion of emotions
will be unstoppable.

## *Pop the Champagne*

I wasn't meant to have a life
filled with 8 am wake-up calls
and 5 pm drives home
during rush hour.
I was meant to have
a life filled with
unexpected mornings that lead to
unforgettable nights.
And even if right now I eat cheap
take out three nights a week,
one day I will be toasting
with overpriced champagne
to a life I knew
I was meant to lead.

I was a people watcher.
Looking on with
eyes that longed
for the lives I was watching
unfold in front of me.
The lives that looked
so perfect on the surface.
But if I pushed back her
hair, I would see bruises
on her neck.
If I shifted my eyes to
the right, I would see
a boyfriend's grip on her
extra tight.
And maybe she was looking
back at me,
with eyes that longed
to be where I stood.
Safe.

The problem with being
sentimental
is that the breakup
is only the beginning
of the hurt.
Replacing his sweatshirt
that you wore
on chilly days,
that smelled like
hugs and bar soap,
was like ripping out
another chunk of your heart.
But I promise you,
the next sweatshirt will
feel better,
smell better,
love better,
than the one before.

**-you will find the one**

I put my feet in the grass
and am thankful
to know it is green,
and soft but sometimes
burned by the sun and crunchy.
I am thankful to know
what it feels like to be
a living thing needing
so little,
to happily survive.

If I could,
I would dip my fingers
in the sun,
and smear its brightness
around the world.

*-we need it*

## *Wandering Soul*

You have a wandering soul
that is searching for a place
to call home.
Flying with the wings of
your heart.
Looking for a location
to land on.
For an attentive spirit to
capture your bad thoughts
and turn them into
healthy ones.
But his arms spread wide open
aren't a place to come in for
landing.
He wants to listen in order to
further his advantage
of getting into more than just
your mind.
Your wandering soul needs
to find a home within yourself.
Take time to rest and glide.

Jennae Cecelia

## *Letting People Go*

It's hard to let go of people.
We anchor ourselves to their flesh.
We grow to love their smile,
laugh, sense of humor,
and the familiarity
of their presence.
It's not until we start to do the
little things that we feel the pain
of their absence.
Like late afternoon card games
with an empty seat,
lunches at the place you both loved
but can no longer enjoy,
and one-sided conversations
with them even though they have
a lot to say back.
A glimpse at life without them is sad.
But you know they don't find home
here anymore,
so feel free to let their spirit fly.

They say, "you look amazing,"
but they can't see inside your head.

*-looks are deceiving*

I hope one day you realize
the only enemy you should
give attention to
is the one inside your head.

*-you are your own worst enemy*

We get caught up in the idea
that the only way
we can be fully happy is
if our bodies look like
what we've always dreamt
for them to be.
But didn't you ever hear
of all the people who go broke,
even after winning the lottery?

You can pluck me
like a dandelion and
hope I never come back.
But I always do.

*-I am a beautiful weed*

Have confidence in the shape
of your silhouette,
the thoughts you share,
and the blood in your veins.
The person picking apart
every little flaw
is not them,
it's you.

*-confidence is beautiful*

## *Nailed*

1 nail in each foot.
Pinning you in place.
No pivot,
no escape.
Take out your nails,
with the claws you enable.
The scars will heal.
Holes will be filled.
Goodbye to you,
the mannequin.

I found love in sheets wrinkled
around his body as I lay next to him.
The way that he called me
six different nicknames
but never once called me
a harsh name out of anger.
I found love in the way he drove
two hours with his hand in mine
every moment,
to surprise me with a gift he
researched for in secret.
In the way he never left me feeling
uncertain about what we were.
The way that I was his,
he was mine,
and we were us.
Together.
He called us a team.
I believe everyone needs a teammate.
One who supports you,
and isn't trying to compete
against you as an opposing rival.

You can't change me
like a popped tire
or, a cracked window
I am not physically broken.
You have to learn that
my mental health isn't just
a simple five-step repair.

*-all I need is your support*

Some days I feel like I am
physically present
on this earth
with every other human,
but my mind is in
a zone that is way
out of this world.

## *Command Your Passion*

Your clock begins to slowly tick
towards the end.
Your breaths become less frequent.
Your heart is beating at a decreased rate.
Think of the life that you have created.
How do you feel about that life?
Did you accomplish your dreams?
Did your bucket list have
items crossed off or was that just the,
"maybe one day, I don't know" list?
Were you fair to yourself and
your passions?
Are your grandchildren going to
tell stories about your life
long after you're gone?
YOU need to be doing what you love.
You NEED to be doing what you love.
You need to be doing what you LOVE.
Don't do it for the ones demanding
from you.
Do it for you.
Don't get stuck in the mindset that
you are no more than the people
who raised you or the place
you were born.
This world isn't made of eggshells.
Stomp on the ground and
command your passion.

You are toes deep
in the water.
Let me pull you out
into the sea of uncertainty.
I promise I won't let you go
until you are ready to
swim on your own with ease.

While the world sleeps,
I accomplish my dreams.
While the world sleeps,
I sit and watch the sun appear
above the tree lines.
While the world sleeps,
I breathe in the silence.
While the world sleeps,
I rise.

You are always
the first to tell yourself
that you aren't beautiful,
smart,
or kind.
You are always the first
to beat up your mind.
You take people's complements
and throw them to the ground
with the thought that you can't
be any of those things.
But you can,
you are.
Beauty,
intelligence,
and kindness
run through your veins.

I held you close to my ear
like I did with a seashell
as a child,
in hopes of helping me
hear the ocean.
I always longed to
hear the parts of you
that seemed so far away.

## *Take Time To Yourself*

Take time for yourself.
It is not lazy to stop the pen
from flowing for a day.
To put down your phone
and ignore answering
business emails.
To take a day to reply back
to messages or calls from friends.
Read a book,
shop online,
or take a long bath
with candles lit.
Taking time for you is healthy.
Your mind needs a break from
the hustle of your busy life.
Don't feel bad for taking moments
to yourself.
Spending a day away from
kids or peers.
Spend a day alone with only
your thoughts.

Negativity is a chain reaction
virus that only ends
in devastation.
The problem is,
only a few are vaccinated.

Second chances exist
but I stopped handing
them out
to the people who kept
coming back for
the third,
fourth,
and fifth time
and expected me
to welcome them
with an open mind
and warm arms.

You can be a Queen
without a King
and still
run the world
just fine on your own.

Seek out the positivity
in your life.
Even if everything around you
seems shitty,
search for the one thing that isn't.
It will save you.

I think October 18
sounds like a good day
to start making change
in your life.
Like the leaves on the trees
and the drop in temperature.

## *Caged*

I felt bad for the bird
in its cage that would
look out through its bars
at the blue sky
and trees.
I, too, felt like
I was looking out at
something I wanted but
couldn't reach.
Until you,
you were the one
to set me free.

## *Resolutions*

5, 4, 3, 2, 1......
The clock ticks down
to a time yet begun.
Pens tracing paper with ink
bleeding ambition
and new beginnings.
A kiss to seal a pressed envelope
filled with hope.
Resolutions have a stigma of failing.
Starting with full force and then
crashing in catastrophe.
Don't wait until December 31
to start being or doing what
it is you dream of.
Pretend there is no recollection
of time at all.
Just start,
and don't be sad
if at first it doesn't work.
Start over the next day.
That's the beauty of life,
we have every day to
gain and be better.

## *Your Words*

If the words that spewed
out of your mouth
were the clothes wrapped
around your body,
the hair on your head,
the flesh of your skin,
would you think you are beautiful?

Don't wake up
at six when
school starts at eight,
if all you are trying to
do is impress
someone
who doesn't give
two shits about
your thoughts,
let alone your hair.

I was a diary
with a lock that could only
be accessed with a key.
Hiding safe under a pillow
from the hands that
tried to pry me open.
You didn't need to break into
me because you were patient
enough to be granted access.

How amazing it is
to now listen to songs
with blissful lyrics
and not feel sad for my
own lack of happiness.

I am itching for highways
that lead to unknown destinations.
People I may only encounter for hours
but change my life for years.
I am an open road,
head out the window,
eyes wide open.

I think about you holding
me close on our wedding day.
I dreamt of the moment
two hands would wrap
around my waist.
I never knew what to envision
those hands looking like.
Would they be white,
black,
tan,
scared,
soft,
callused?
All I cared about was that
they were the type of hands
that would touch me
beautifully and carefully.
Even on the days we
didn't dance to the same beat.
We would always find our footing
back to the place we met.

## *Make Yourself Happy*

People may question
your happiness.
People may hate
your happiness.
People may embrace
your new-found happiness.
At least people are noticing
that happiness is in your life.

Jennae Cecelia

## *Forgive Yourself*

It's time to forgive your old self
for the days you put
harm on your body,
placed negative thoughts
in your mind,
and pushed your
dreams away.
It's time to thank your old self
for teaching you
the love you deserve,
for recognizing
the positive vs. the negative,
and for giving you strength.
You have a past that is daunting
to think about,
but your future is glowing.

You could work your life
at a job you hate for
money that's guaranteed.
Or, you can live your life
in the way you would choose
to love, and be guaranteed
leaving the world with a
smile on your face
and no regrets.

*-I will regret nothing*

I see the world in the
eyes of the explorers,
the dreamers,
the wanderers.
Let me show you
the beauty
through my eyes.

*-open your eyes and your heart*

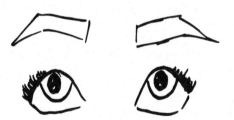

How beautiful it is
that I no longer write
with sorrow
at the beginning
of every sentence
and still have so much
to write about.

My heart aches for
your pain because
I know how it feels
to bleed
and have no one
to be your Band-Aid.

## *The Best*

Life isn't about
always being the best.
It's about facing fears and
growing from them.
You don't have to be number one.
Just don't live a life full of,
"what if's."

## *New Soil*

Life will always have
horrible moments.
Moments you want to cry
into your pillow
and scream out the agony
that you've buried inside.
But there are always
more radiant days ahead.

Life may throw dirt on you,
but it's up to you to see
the good to come.
Grow in your new soil with
beams of happiness,
do not drown in tears.

## Dear You,

You made it.
You are here.
All the moments spent in agony,
wondering when the pain
would end and,
you are here.
You made it.
Your mind is beautiful
and brilliant.
You may not be everyone's
cup of tea,
some people need cream
or sugar just to take you.
Others enjoy you pure in taste.
But neither of that matters,
because you are at a place
you once dreamed of as your escape.
Who knew you would love smiling,
pure, genuine smiles that didn't
hint at the firing thoughts behind
your eyes.
You want others to know that
their minds can feel
this wonderful too.
We made it my friend.
Now it's time for your breakthrough.

## *Comfort Zone*

One life.
Many stories
to make.
A comfort zone
should no longer
hold you in place.

## *Journey*

Life is a journey,
full of wonder and worry,
but today I am at peace.
My mind will no longer
over-analyze the past, or
stress about the unknown ahead.
I am present in the moments
in front of my eyes.

Every day you get the chance
to work on being
the version of yourself
that you would be excited
to meet for coffee.

## *My Mind*

I used to think my mind
must be made up of
storm clouds,
lightning,
flooded rain,
and thunder.
But you helped me realize
what I truly embodied:
green grass,
sunshine,
blue skies,
crisp air.
Some days, there are still
sprinkles of rain
and a cloud or two.
But I am no longer near
that awful typhoon.

I cheer for
the people who try.
Who try and better themselves.
Who try and give back.
Who try loving themselves.
Who try appreciating others.
I cheer for the people who try.
Because trying is half the battle.

## *Feelings*

I used to fight tears
like they were lions
pouncing at me from a cage.
Biting my tongue so hard it bled,
because tears meant weakness
and that wasn't okay.
I remember the feeling
of a hard lump
stuck in my throat from
sucking in so much air
just to make sure no
water could escape.
My body was flooding itself
with unshed tears.
Like a dam that was
soon to break.
Tears showed weakness.
Weakness.
I am weak.
I never knew tears
were normal.
Tears made me bleed.

You can tend to me
like a tree
entangled with
telephone wires,
but I will always
end up branching
out on my own.

## She Is Spring

She is now who she always
envisioned being.
The person in the reflection of
bodies of water and
mirrors on the walls is
no longer unrecognizable.
She looks just as she feels.
Her soul illuminates through
her skin.
The hate she once embodied
has overgrown to love.
Like a garden never weeded,
she is the flower budding
from the ground.
She is the grass that turned
from singed brown
to soft green.
She is the spring
right after winter.

## *I Am Better Now*

I know that if you saw me now,
you would recognize me.
You wouldn't turn your head
in surprise.
There would be no lift
of your eyebrow.
What you wouldn't
recognize though,
is that same girl
laughing and smiling.
I am no longer a victim.
I am no longer your puppet.
I am no longer the girl
you could reach out to
and know you would receive
a quick response.
I hated the person
you turned me into.
Today I am strong.
Today I am worthy.
Today I am successful.
I don't hate you, though.
Because hate is a feeling and
I feel nothing for you.

I'm neither fat
nor skinny.
I'm just cells
protecting my inner
most important things.
Like my beautiful brain
and big heart.

*-I'm made up of love and kindness*

She made art
from the parts of her
that were broken.
She finds beauty in chaos.

We are all works in progress.
The first draft of a book.
The blueprints of a house.
The child learning to read.

We are all works in progress.
We choose to finish writing out
a story untold,
building a house out of
bricks and wood
that once started out as ideas
on paper,
and reading chapter books
with ease late into the night.

We are all works in progress.
Slowly but surely coming together.
We are the ones who never give up.

Jennae Cecelia

I put honey in
my bitter tea to make it
a little sweeter,
if only I could do
the same with you.

*-poetry can be honey to your tea*

You are a broken
bone that needs to heal.
Let my words be the cast
you wear to
return you
to your best form.

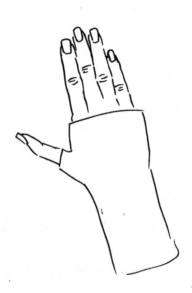

There are many
types of people who get
together for coffee.
Some who gossip
about friends as they
sip up the foam
from their espresso.
Some who get together
and talk about
how they are accomplishing
their dreams while
their coffee
sits and gets cold.
Which one would you be?

## *I Am My Own Competition*

The person I was last year
is not the person I am this year.
I am always in a competitive game.
A faster,
better,
stronger mentality.
Not competing with anyone
except for the girl I was yesterday.

## *Love Me Big*

I am not a 4 a.m. phone call
when no one else is awake.
I am a 5 p.m. knock at the door
after you sat in rush hour traffic
just to tell me you love me.

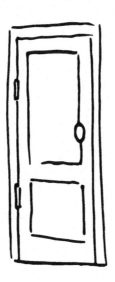

## *Use Your Voice*

There are so many beautiful people on
this earth that I won't ever have the
privilege of meeting,
but know that your voice
holds the power to
impact the masses.

## *Dreams*

Be your dreams;
don't talk about them.
Don't see them as out of reach.
Don't mock them.
Don't allow others to bring
your dreams down.
Live, and breathe your dreams.

I am no longer the one
falling apart.
I am the one walking around
trying to pick up
everyone else's pieces.

**-I want you to be happy**

I didn't wait around for
you to bring your
portion to the table.
I set the scene tonight
for me and good company
and you were not invited.

When I break you down
to the simplest form,
like an acoustic song,
I find you the most beautiful.

I know that
the opposite ends
of magnets
attract and attach
to one another.
Positive + Negative.
But I can guarantee that
won't work for you and me.

*-positive + positive*

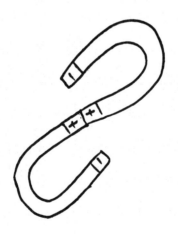

I told myself that I deserve the best,
so that is what I set out for.
Never settling for anything less
just to fit into the
cookie cutter mold.
Because of that all my,
"crazy" dreams,
are coming to fruition.
You deserve the best too.

*-no one can believe in you more than yourself*

Dreams are meant to be chased
not buried in fear.

*-get running*

I'm still learning
to love myself more
each day.
You are not alone on
your self-love journey.

I have changed a lot over
the last year and a half.
I have grown,
learned,
and expanded who I am.
If we no longer align,
it is what it is.

This physical life
you lead here on earth
is supposed to be
your time to make
your impact on the world.
Don't let things like limitations
stop you from leading
your best life here.

Jennae Cecelia

I am taxiing down a runway
that has been going on
far too long.
I am looking for a sign
to take off,
but I am starting to think
I should stop worrying
about a sign
and just fly.

## *Beauty Comes In All Forms*

Learn to be your own
beautiful self while also
recognizing that there are many
other people who carry
beauty too.
There is no need
for competition.

Here you are, 23
with your dream career,
dream partner in life,
dream mindset.
You showed
your 16-year-old self,
just how wrong
she was.

*-I showed you*

If you call to the Universe
and tell it
you are ugly,
you are tired,
you are sick,
you are broken,
you are poor,
you are lazy,
you are bad.
The Universe will echo
what it hears.

If you call to the Universe
and tell it,
you are beautiful,
you are woke,
you are healthy,
you are strong,
you are wealthy,
you are good.
The Universe will echo
what it hears.

Don't you see,
the Universe is giving you
what you emit.
Be more cautious of your words.

Jennae Cecelia

What happened to that
five-year-old dreamer
that lived inside of you?
The doctor,
the dentist,
the lawyer,
the singer.
Who made you forget
about those dreams?
Who made you feel like
you couldn't be those things?

He says he likes the dimples
on your face,
but does he love the ones
on your thighs
just as much?

*-you are cute in every way*

Jennae Cecelia

### *Sizes*

I would rather be
my size ten
with a mind that loves
my body,
instead of my size four
that beat up my body.

One day we will
look back on the days
that we could barely afford
99 cent tacos,
or more than a couple
gallons of gas.
The days we sat on
folding chairs in our
living room watching
a TV with four channels.
One day we will tuck our kids
in bed in rooms much bigger
than ours ever were.
And thank God every day
because we knew we could get
here.

If I asked you
all the things
that you love about
yourself,
how long would
our conversation be?

You wanted a succulent
that could be left
on the shelf for weeks
without needing any effort.
But I am a rose in a garden
that needs maintaining,
and tending to my needs
was too much work for you.

I used to be composed of
"maybe"
and "I'm sorry,"
out of fear of commitment
or being an inconvenience.
But now, I will tell you
straight as it is,
and only apologize
if I truly did
something wrong.

I know you say
that I will be nothing
without you,
but I am already
slipping into
a cloak of invisibility
with you.

*-it's time to break free*

No emotion is permanent.
You don't always have
to be happy
to be okay.
Sometimes being sad
is just what
your mind needs
in the moment.

*-it's alright to cry*

Flowers grow back
even after the harshest winters,
you will too.

Jennae Cecelia

It's funny how people love
the mountains,
the flowers,
and trees.
Things that come
in all different sizes.
But for some reason,
we see beauty in people
who are shorter than the trees,
and skinner than the mountains.
When really everyone
who is tall,
short,
round,
square,
are all just a beautiful part of
nature we have yet to appreciate.

Be above the hate you see.
The hate you feel.
The hate you give.
Be above the hate
that is standing tall.

Today, do you for.
Don't wear what
you think others will like.
Don't talk about
what you think others
want to hear.
Do for you today.

## *Socialize In Real Life*

Focus more time on building
the relationships you have
in your real life
and put the social media
relationships on the
back burner.
Don't let your online life control
how you live your life
outside of a screen.
You are missing so much.

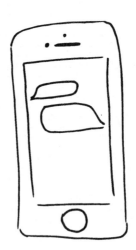

It's the middle of fall.
The temperature has dipped
below a bone-chilling 40 degrees.
I have on my big gray sweater that
I bought back in the 12 grade.
The one I wore as a safety
blanket for when my anxiety
would creep in.
I can still run my thumbs
over the cuffs of the sleeves,
to the places I used to chew at
out of eagerness.
It's small moments like these
that remind me of
how far I have come.
How I now just wear this sweater
to keep warm and not because
I saw it as my escape.

I know we all
hate the days
when the sun disappears
in the early hours of the evening.
Just remember, like us,
everything needs a break
once and awhile.

Does he text you,
"good morning (insert nickname),"
every morning?
Does he praise you for
your victories
and hold your hand through
your sorrows?
Are your success'
as important as his?
Does he make you feel safe?
Don't allow yourself to think
that you only deserve half of
those things,
or one of them.
You deserve them all.
Nothing should be forced.
He should love you naturally.

Forget trying to impress
the rest of the world,
the first person you need to
impress is yourself.

*-do you know how amazing you are?*

### *You Are Magnificent*

Take yourself to breakfast,
treat yourself
to freshly picked flowers.
Go on a date with yourself
and learn about just how
magnificent you are.

Women carry
the most beauty in
their thoughts.
Where is the song
about her gorgeous
mind and not how
her humps look?

Jennae Cecelia

Anxiety is the panic
you feel when
someone doesn't answer
your phone call after
five tries.
Are they okay?
Did they lose their phone?
Are they mad at me?
Did someone take them?
Are they sick?
Anxiety is never rationalizing
that they could have fallen asleep
or walked away from their phone.
Anxiety is worse case scenario.

A flower missing a few petals
is still just as beautiful
as the flower with an
abundance of petals
but is pulled out at the roots.

*-beauty comes in every form*

Jennae Cecelia

If you were a flower in a garden,
which one would you be?
I would be a sunflower
because they stand tall,
need the sun's rays,
and room to breathe.

Maybe you are waiting for Saturday,
or summer time,
or New Year's Eve
to start living out your dream.
But I started in the middle of debt
and anxiety and I was victorious.

*-no time is ever perfect*

It isn't about waiting for
life to get better.
It is about believing that
life is the best it is right now.
That is when you see
the transformation
in your life.

I don't want you to think
that I am perfect,
because I am not.
I cry,
scream,
and fear
just like you.

*-I'm human*

Run with me
through fields filled
with prosperity
and happiness.
I promise you will
not miss the
barren desert
you once called home.

I know that last thing
I would have wanted to hear
was, "things will get better."
But they do.
They get better,
you get stronger,
and you learn what life
was truly trying to offer you
was the experience you needed
to conquer any demons
who may cross your path again.

I hope my future daughter
doesn't have to resort to
social media to find her worth,
and vent about her problems.
I want her to know
she always has me to come to.

Helping others is
nice of you,
but I noticed
the bags under your eyes
and the twitching
from over-indulging in caffeine.
You need to be kind
to yourself too.

The imagination of a child
stems far beyond
that of an adult.
That is because
they haven't learned yet
that there'd be
outside opinions tainting
their dreams.
So, be the child in you,
and make your imagination
a place in your reality.

Flood this world
with so much love
that the hate can
barely stay breathing.

I may be a quiet person
but it is because I only
speak words that are
true to me,
and not words
I feel forced into saying
to fit into the conversation.

I put the girl I was to rest
3 years ago today.
I don't mourn her loss
because she was never
alive anyway.

**-born again**

I think we all fear
losing someone we love,
which is why we limit
gaining someone to love.

Friend groups shrink
as you grow.
There is nothing wrong
with that.

Jennae Cecelia

I write for the dreamers,
and the strong believers,
that we can conquer
our demons,
while wearing flowers
in our hair
and smiles on our faces.

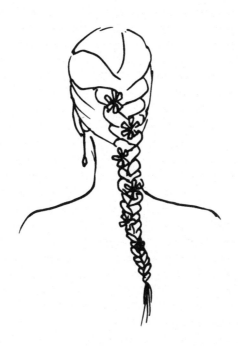

If you told me five years ago
that I would be promoting
positivity and chasing dreams,
I would have never
believed you.
I write for the "me"
five years ago,
and for all of you who are or
have been in a similar mindset.
I saved her,
and I hope I can help you, too.
Thank you for always
believing in me.

Jennae Cecelia

## *About the Author*

JennaeCecelia.com

Instagram/Twitter: @JennaeCecelia


Jennae Cecelia is the self-published and best-selling author of the poetry books, *Bright Minds Empty Souls, Uncaged Wallflower* and *I Am More Than a Daydream.*

The revised and expanded edition of *Uncaged Wallflower* marks her fourth book.

She has developed a strong passion for writing uplifting poetry that encourages her readers to reach their full potential and learn about fulfilling their dreams.

CPSIA information can be obtained
at www.ICGtesting.com
Printed in the USA
LVOW13s2103060318
568848LV00015B/1518/P